My Last Everything

by

Joel Duncan

THE KING'S ENGLAND PRESS

2015

ISBN 978-1-909548-53-4

MY LAST EVERYTHING
is typeset in
Book Antiqua and Gill Sans
and published by
The King's England Press
111 Meltham Road
Lockwood
HUDDERSFIELD
West Riding of Yorkshire

Printed and bound in Great Britain by
Lulu Press Inc, digital print on demand

My Last Everything

I dedicate this book to my writing group
"Igniting The Spark".
Before them, all I had was imagination
and a far-fetched goal.

Contents

FEAR To Speak

We panic first
Then think too late,
But that's the worst mistake
Anyone could possibly make!

You open your mouth
With so much to say,
Then our minds go wandering
once people are looking our way.

They tell you all the time
"Don't worry you'll be fine"
But they don't say why,
That's the biggest crime.

Think of your fear.
Got it?
If you read carefully here,
There's an easy way to stop it.

Look at it this way
You're a character inside your own brain,
If you can change the story of your fear
Will the end be the same?

We are attempting to predict our future
We are trying to guess our own fate,
But these things are just the products of our imagination
An idea we must learn to hate.

Think about the person you want to be,

Create the visual sensations that you want to see.
That's your future,
Until it's a memory in the past.
Soon you will realise
Your fear's gone,
just as fast.

Unread

One buzz or two?
One bump or two?
Two mistakes and you're dead.
Don't get into the mind-set
the next car crash won't be you
just because it hasn't happened yet.
Whoever has phoned when you're in the
car all alone can wait until you get home or
wherever you're going.
A quick read may leave red paint
on the pavement.
Parents bereaved.
A text never received.

2009

I met you.

the truth
the brute

when I didn't know
what to do

you pulled me
through.

The clue
I knew
I needed to find

although
I didn't know

at the time it was right
in front of my eyes.

I love you.

An Impossible Moment

I said goodbye.
Even though I'd revised the
plan too many times,
I still stepped into a minefield.
Or should I say mind-field?
Because the thoughts and feelings
I'd mapped out precisely were
Exploding all over my body and I
Didn't know which one to
cling onto next.

After we separated I was starving.
The only food I could manage was
A thought of nibbling on her
Bottom lip like I used to.
I felt like melting wax and pouring
The corpses of candles into my
ears so the only thing I'd hear
was the echo of 'I love you' still
bouncing around my hollow skull.

But one day she came around.
Beginning, middle and end didn't
fit our story any more; it needed a
new label.
We sat down on the couch and dug
around for our souls that had left our
bodies and were sulking somewhere
in the shadows of what we once had.

Gravity took an unexpected twist and
I could feel the hold I had on the arm of
the chair losing its grip.
We found ourselves touching fingertips.
I swear enough electric ran down my
arms, I could have killed a small mouse.
My heart was causing an earthquake; I was
surprised I didn't bring down the house.

Then there was a kiss I'd been wishing
For, even though it was me that cut
off the relationship, there's something
now that's magnetic.

I guess you do only know you truly
Love her when you let her go.
But you must be prepared for the
Holes that will follow.

April Tools

I had a few sandwiches missing
from the picnic basket back then.
At school there would have
been mayhem if I had found my sense
before twelve o'clock, but of course,
like always, I was the victim.
When the predators came I curled up
in a corner instead of bit them.

I saw three lads walking towards me,
ready to torment my brain until it

became stupidly paranoid.
These pieces of dirt were hard
to avoid in a small building.
My brain was sticky and clung
to insults and bad thoughts,
but my heart was hard steel
and had to unlearn all the
negativity my brain was taught.

The memory is as clear
as the air I breathe.
"Have you polished your forehead?
It's really shiny!
Why would you do something
like that, are you trying to blind me?"

The rest of the day I tried to rub
the shine from my face.
It's a nightmare that repeatedly plays.
It was a prank done in spite for April fools
Committed by a group of April tools.

But, today,
bullying and lies
I've known all my life
have stood up and mysteriously
disappeared into the horizon.

Zombie In The Cupboard

A laptop like a graveyard for bugs
sits on my lap topped with dust and
an electrical charge of excitement.
But I can't excite it back to life.
Where's the charger?
I charge into every room
searching for the device's lifeline,
it's a blind obstacle course.
Might as well try and find
a grain of sand in a haystack.
My body sack isn't stacked with
patience and it must be fraying
because it's pouring out of me.
I pour myself a drink and think.
It's probably in the only place
I haven't searched.
Hastily placed in the cupboard
with the zombie.
I don't think the idiom 'skeleton
In the closet' describes how
dark the secrets I've stashed
in there are.
I grab the charger from the
sleeping zombie's ribs before
it has a chance to munch on mine.
I stab the tip into the laptop
like a knife in the stomach.
I'm ready to stomach what is
on there, it feels like an awakening.
I tap in the keys to my password
like the beat of a familiar tune.

The laptop downloaded all my
emotions and left me numb
When I noticed everything I'd left
for my future self to discover
had gone.

Astronaut

The bedroom floats in space,
connecting to life is complicated.
I am frustrated because the books
don't speak to me anymore.
The only bedtime stories told
are the nonsense my
dreams show me.
I have one small window
of opportunity,
Another doesn't open at all.
Cushions make up for the empty
space and keep me company.
Some memories are dead and
I've stored them under my bed.
Blank pages whisper from the
drawers in the corner to ink their skins.
Stars that are supposed to light up
my room don't work anymore,
they have began to gather star dust.
Then there's me the astronaut.
Gazing through the small cracks in
the walls,
preparing to take off someday
but I'm not quite there yet.

Under The Magnifying Glass

Everything I used to do had to be magnified,
as if I was incapable of getting anything right.
But then I was under a pressure I couldn't manage.
I kept so much anger pent-up I'm surprised I
didn't give myself brain damage.

I always said and did the wrong things and
each one was like a brick that constructed
multiple buildings -
failure skyscrapers .
You couldn't even spot my achievements
from up there.
Even when I'd swallowed the fact an apology
wouldn't act as a way to get along,
I realised that people who blamed me when
anything went wrong would have to have been
young and dumb to be old and wise.

Every mistake I committed had to
be in some way outwitted.
The errors greeted them like a stranger
even though they have probably met
face to face before.

I don't know why I even started to write,
I guess I took to the fact all the art ever
asked me to do was try.

Auto-drive

Self-driving cars are the hype now,
I'm living in that movie I watched as a child.
When they told me anything was possible
I'd want to nod my head,
But my fingers would cross instead.

I would always wish for the day to end
before it had even begun.
Pretend I was having fun just so time
would grow wings and take flight.
I lived life in slow motion.
If only there was a potion to crystallize
the precious moments of my high school romance.
I would place it on my shelf like an ornament.
 Let me know if you find a remote
to rewind back to the time when
problems were too minor to care about.

I admit,
if you leave auto-drive to control your life
You might just get used to it.

Your Opinion Based On Mine

You probably see me as a confident person,
But I'm actually bubble wrap ready to pop
as soon as somebody applies any pressure.
I worsen it because the version I see of you
is a human spell checker highlighting every
mistake I make with a permanent red marker.

I watch politics like a child watching Pinocchio,
Wondering if their strings will snap or if some
Politian's nose has grown.
You may gaze at them through the TV waiting for
them to rip open their specially woven suits and fly
our economy into a financial growth like superheroes.

Jesus is a nonchalant genie who is supposed to grant
Us wishes and because he's all so powerful it must be easy.
He can't be real because I've never seen a miracle.
People actually think this way, they staple that logic to
Their foreheads like the headline of a newspaper.
I think our guardian angels are watching over us as
We clamber into a slingshot.
God has to pull us back hard before he
can propel to the stars.

Sometimes I believe I am wasting my time,
Writing rhymes that nobody's ever going to read.
But you disagree and say "you're doing it for me".
A wise man told me once that I was never afraid to
Step across the line with poetry and he loved that.
But he didn't know I am always ready to jump back.

Spill the Ink

The universe of my words start with the stars.
Flickering lights humans gaze upon and
Admire, love or hate because there's too many.

My story will be no different.

Pin your finger on one planet.
Earth.
The globe is our beating heart
that keeps us breathing.
But still we disobey and try to escape
with rockets, space stations, black holes
that suck in the interest of astronauts.
We wish to explore where nobody has
been before.

These are my ideas.

Travel the world and you will see
Trees, animals and the veins of rivers
running into the sea.
They are everywhere, ignored.
Although some choose to study their mark,
They try to find the meaning of life
and how it all started.

My dying wish.

We are left with you and me.
The most complex beings of all.
So why do I understand

humans the most?
More than I should or want to.
Treasure chest filled with personalities,
experiences and goals.

We are characters
and the memories we make are
stories in themselves.

X Marks The Killer

There's no method we can use to
illuminate a predator in the darkness
of our gloomy world.
It's not like they were born to do this.
When kids flood your ears with fantasy
jobs like becoming a bird, princess or a superhero.
There was never one that would cuddle the
corner of the classroom and tell everyone they
wanted to be a paedophile.
There is a spark of love in every twisted mind,
but sometimes it's love itself that transforms them
into an uncontrollable beast to feast
on the innocent or virgins that fall into
their claws.
But when evil creeps up their spines and snaps
off the morality switches in their minds,
there's not a single clock that can count
down the time until their first crime.
I'm not saying they can't control it.
There's just fear burning my stomach like
acid because I know there evil inside us all.

Spell evil backwards and tell me we'll one
day inhabit an evil deprived world.

Birdman

He gazed at a flock of birds.
Resting upon a rock cloud on the mountain top
inspired by their characteristics.
The sky's army has conquered
the world all in unison but now their recycling life
has commanded them to do it all again.
They're so nonchalant.
No restraints forcing their feet to roam
the same old streets wishing
For a change in scenery.

A bird swoops and watches the
Cinematic view just as he was.
The minutes became cannibals
And started to eat themselves.
Still unsatisfied when hours came
by they devoured them too.
Both readied to leave but you
Couldn't be sure who
would take flight first.

Black Box

Wanting to forget is truly a strange feeling.
You cast your memory-maggots out to sea,
hoping to reel something beautiful back in return.
But what if you don't forget, but instead store them away?
Like wine laying amid the others in the cortex-cellar,
Aging and maturing into something so intensely flavoured,
it's indescribable.
Perhaps you've messed with what could possibly be the most
valuable bottle you hold.
So instead when you finally pop the cork,
you are left with a bitter taste that claws at your tongue.

I have a black box.
The tick-tocks of five years are secreted inside,
along with an abundance of treasured memories.
I can pat myself on the back,
my intrusive behaviour is in restraints.
I am only a shuddering-sure about one thing,
a naïve letter waits for the same person who wrote it,
to open it back up again.

Childish words marked onto paper,
Play the guessing game of the future.
But I guess guessing is part of our nature.
We wander through the labyrinth of time,
sometimes we think there is a route we haven't
stumbled upon yet.
A way out of the darkness.
But most of the time this exit is right in front,
however we fail to see it in the bewilderment
of the many paths to take.

It isn't possible to warn yourself what the next
distant decades will bring,
just as impossible as trying to fill an empty memory.
So before you strap your memories to a rocket
that has a target destination of a black hole.
Stop. Breathe. Think.

Become your own hero.
Forget about forgetting.
Store everything your heart knows is important,
Because one day you will understand.

A Swinging Portrait

She hung flaccidly.
I passed her by like I was just a small
child that wanted to dabble in the
game of love for a while.

She was my long distance oxygen.
Always there, until she wasn't.
Breathing became a complex
math problem,
That I never found the solution for.

I carry a load twice my weight,
Others offered to take some,
But this was my mistake.
They have taken her away,
Hung her on a new wall,
A crumbling mess that lets so much

dust fall onto the glass,
I no longer see her face.
My thoughts loiter in an empty space
I am now locked out of.
Creative waste just leaks
From it now and again.

My love should have never
graced her with its presence.
I wish at school they would have
taught me how to be more evanescent.

Woven

When she was depressed,
her heart would sink so low it was in her toes.
It made it hard to stand on her own two feet.
She would sleep with sheets full of waste,
because she couldn't face her
uncompleted bedroom.

She could have filled the bath with her tears
from how many years she cried.
Love hadn't stayed by her side,
so her sleep routine died.
The sun didn't rise anymore,
she had lost the concept of time.

Her smiling muscles had frozen.
Everything felt hopeless.
Faith was woven into her
but she had torn some holes

without knowing.

God sewed them back up.
He told her he might let her
bend but never break.
Her life was stuck in a rut.
The weight of the world is heavy,
but he knew she was strong enough
to take it.

Why

I'd question everything, like 'why'was
the only word in the dictionary.
My mind would have a picture of
the answer but it would be blurry
like puddle water so I'd hope people
would jump into it and soak me with
the knowledge that's too cloudy.
But some things never
become clear, do they?

I used to think I was incapable
of winning anything.
But then why did I finish first
in the race to my mother's egg?
Why does life keep handing
me these one way tickets
that lead to dead ends?
I always end up a train wreck.
Why is there a stranger trying
To copy my every move?

I'm not even suitable to be
A role model to
My own reflection.

I'm constantly stuck on record,
Every word crams itself into my mouth
and gets stuck inbetween my teeth.
I think I just was put on this earth to
question everything,
I guess most of them I could already answer
but I fear that would be more like a confession.
Displaying my life's thoughts and feelings on the
wall like a movie at the cinema.
I don't want you to think I'm a
walking contradiction.

Body Bag

I don't need a rucksack because I am filled
with the things that make me who I am.
My poetry is stashed inside my cranium,
sometimes it escapes through the hole in
my mouth because I talk for so long and
so loud other topics of conversation are
wearing now so it just keeps on slipping out.

My heart is packed to the brim with love,
there's no space to shove hate in.
Though with other emotions trying to twist
into the corners like contortionists I feel
like it's going to bust and leak anger
into my fists and my knees will wish

nervousness never came to exist.

I don't carry the problems that have sunk
to the bottom of other people's rucksacks
and I don't need to carry around a road map
to my life, believe me I have tried that.
Every time I asked someone else for
directions they got me lost.
It's one of my imperfections,
to rely on other people.
I eventually get to my destination,
but at what cost?
Years of my life have passed by
and the whole time I was looking at
the wrong signs or maybe I just paid
a sculptor to chisel away my pride.

Ever since the opportunity arose
I've been tossing lost memories to
my toes, they've been sitting there
on my bone-pews waiting for
God to shine some light on them.

Voodoo

I stuff the doll with hands that groan,
tired from hammering nails into the
structure of my will power just to stop
it from collapsing on top of me.
The wire stitching that runs through
the body of your doll could have
happily been used to strangle the air
from me, but your words do the same job.
I tattoo your face in the space on its head
in permanent ink so you know this feeling I have
to want to hear you screaming in fear will never pass.

Now where should I stab this broken piece of glass?
In the eyes that harassed my confidence until
I handed it over like some money that I owed you.
Or drive it through the stomach as I watch you
plummet to the ground and I'd thrive from the fact
your bowing to me now.

The best thing about me is that I'm not you,
I'm neither evil or deceitful.
Your minds stuck in a state where you believe
because you haven't achieved anything yet that
nothing is achievable.
The fact I've done what you said was impossible
has made us equal on the scales of how much
pain we've caused each other.
So have this glass back from your smashed
vodka bottle, I don't need it any longer.

Halifax

Welcome to:

The town of forgotten power.
The town of remembered pain.
The town of luminescent fields.
The town of flickering fame.
The town of lost rumours.
The town of found remains.
The town of picturesque landscapes.
The town of ugly mistakes.
The town of drunken tales.
My Town of sober escapes.

Harsh

People that don't look
before they swing,
open my veins
cover themselves with
my crimson ink.

People that look
but still swing
are baneful creatures.
They sever my fragile
heart strings,
tie them to a tree
and hang my body
For all to see.

Piñata

People used to call my friend names,
he would try and laugh it off but they
Stabbed his insecurities until they
Front crawled down his face
and made visible lanes.
Bullies would catch every drop
as if they were dehydrated.
They waited a couple days
After they had caused him pain,
Just to torment him all over again.
He was their piñata filled with
something that must have given

them a sugar rush.
I knew I couldn't let them carry
on beating him with sticks,
but I never have been
good with my fists.
But I could twist words into
A noose and tie it around
Their necks.

Words are so powerful
they can save a life.
He could have took his
Own if I'd just stood by
Even though I could see
The suffering in his eyes.
Bullies will never cease
To exist unless we become
Armour to the weak and
Speak for the ones who's
Tongues have shrivelled
To the back of their throats
And let them know
They never again have
to stand alone.

I Met Love

Love greeted me at the park exit.
She was no stranger.
She had graced me with her presence once before.
I felt my pulse leap.
This time she affected a whole different part of me
I didn't know existed.
My heart beat grew stronger, more ferocious,
pushing against my ribcage hoping for a way to escape.
I closed my eyes as if that would hide me.
The angel of beauty was a luxury you have to witness
for yourself.

Love didn't have to talk to harness my attention
and tie it to her.
Every movement cast a spell on me
that I couldn't shake away.
I already longed to know more about what lay beneath,
I wanted feel what she had felt,
I desired to know what she desired,
I imagined I had travelled
through endless galaxies of emotions
and seen what she had seen.

Love put her hand in mine and smiled,
a smile any man would travel the world to find again.
If you keep her
she will fuel the supernova of passion inside your soul,
but if you let her go,
sleep will not save you.
Memories will haunt you.
Your stable world will fall and collapse in front of you.

Love knows how to win the dangerous game we all play.
Love was a radiant beauty I will never forget.

Purpose

You don't know your purpose?
Time is an attention seeker.
It takes up the limelight every
time you bribe it to skip on a little.
Waiting for the ticks to tock
Will not find your purpose.

It lays in the conversations that you
wish you had a cork to put in your mouth.
Because when you talk about it
You feel like you could explode.
Your knowledge of the topic flows
and makes you drunk on your own words.

Your meaning hides in that opportunity
You thought twice about.
Then you turned it down because of doubt.
It doesn't matter if it shouted from the rooftops
or whispered in your ear.
Sometimes you've already found your purpose,
It's just not clear yet.
Maybe its fear that's blocking you.
Or them so called friends that are stopping you.
In the end nobody is going to die your death for you,
So why should you live a life to suit them?

No matter how impossible your

dream seems,
It's in your blood stream.
Failure is just a stutter in success,
so when the next opportunity comes along
say YES!

Lemons

When life gave me lemons
I would rub their juices into my eyes
and dive head first into the problems others saw coming.
I'd taste their sour complexities and finish my meals
with a bitter feeling inside my heart.
They left me sore,
blinded me from the truth that still lingers
like an undying after taste.

These lemons would be packaged in bags
of five heartbreaks.
The earlier mistakes were easier to devour.
Two remain refrigerated until I am strong enough
to slice them down into pieces and digest them too.

Next time life gives me lemons,
I will drain every last drop and leave it
on the side for you.

White Room

Imagine me and you
sitting in a blank white room,
forget about your life for a moment
and everything you've ever been through.

What's the first question you want to ask?
Why am I here?
Why did you make life disappear?
Why haven't I stopped reading yet,
Is it out of fear?

I know something has happened in your life
and it's making the someone you once were
hide out of sight and out of mind.
Sometimes you may try to blind
yourself from the truth.

But in this white room,
soon you're going to see the light
and fight that pain or else I am going
to hijack your brain and bring you
back here again and again.

If I called you a name in spite,
you wouldn't let it go without a fight.
Because I'm right in front of you and
you can hit me.
Do it now,
I'm your problem so picture you
doing damage.
I am sure I can manage.

Do you know why I am here yet?
I'm here because you're feeding your
scars salt water.
I'm here because you need support
but cast away the people that should be
your bricks and mortar.
I'm here because you have the tools to
rise from the rubble but there's
no instruction manual to life,
that's the trouble.

Though in this room you can be reborn.
Totally start from scratch,
Isn't that thought like brain porn?
Or are you going to stop reading this poem
and tread out into the same storm?

There is a reason why a world wind
has torn through everything you hold on to.
Because you're too strong
and have the power to cling on.
Maybe your hands are sweaty and
you're oozing misery and defeat.
Though it's likely you're the one
choosing misery and defeat.

There's just me and you in this moment.
So throw away fear and doubt right now
and in your head shout like you've
suddenly got a larger mouth
I can do this!
I will do this!

And when I look back in five years
the only regret will be I didn't
do it sooner.

I can only help you in this room.
When you enter back into your life
the only person that can make a change is you
but to achieve that you have to stop
doubting what you can do.

You'll never hear me say it will be easy.
When it becomes too hard to bare,
you know where you can find me.

Notion of Emotion

If emotions were people then fear
would be that person who is certain you will
never achieve your dreams because it's out
of your regular routine.
It will leave a space on the shelves saying
insert awards and medals here.
When failure creeps up your walls,
Fear will come knocking at your door.

Love would be someone that never
Bothers to turn on their phone on at all,
Then immediately pick it up when you call.
They'll catch you even when you've fallen off
the edge of the earth.
They will buy you moon and stars

And give them to you for your birthday
Just to prove you are their universe.

Courage is best friends with fear and love.
It's the hooded figure that stands firm in
the fires of criticism and cruelty.
When you can't take it anymore,
you'll hear his mighty roar and there's
no doubt it will leave you speechless.

Trust is the unstable person in society.
When you gain it you get drunk on
Responsibility, you lose sense of morality
And shower in power and secrets.
If you can keep trust by your side in
tough times it will jump in front of
a bullet for you, trust me.

Blue

Blue is my favourite colour.
But still I ask myself why does everything
in my life have to be out of the blue?
Completely unexpected.
Sometimes success is like a wolf that
howls to a blue moon when it finds you.
Some achievements can be vicious.
Karma is a delicious treat to swallow
if you see the people who laughed when
you were the smallest fish in the ocean,
now they are drowning in their own sorrow.
Don't get me wrong, I've worked hard to be

where I am but everything I've done is to
prove to everyone who sits comfortable in
a boatload of doubt that their ship will sink.
Not every race you enter has to finish
with a blue ribbon.

Love Month

Dear February,

Why are you so small?
You're beautiful and all
but I can't take you seriously
with your boyfriend January
being three days taller than you.

You make me wrap my love twice
for my other half's birthday
and Valentines.
I pray that I'll please her
in the mound of snow
December for months now
has not let go.

I bet the other months think it's funny
to mock how the money
in my bank account
has not grown up yet.

My Last Everything

If I were crashing through the clouds
with no parachute to guide me down.
What would I think about?

If only my younger self had the
knowledge I have now.
Maybe if I knew my end
would come abruptly
stage fright or girls wouldn't stop me.
I wouldn't be afraid to smash
through my comfort zone
and own the world.
I'd keep the globe in my pocket.

My poor mother I left behind
would give her life just to know
I could live the rest of mine.
Yet I couldn't even lift
a finger at home.
She did everything for me
and she managed it on her own.

Would my father do the same?
It's funny but I never knew exactly
what he wanted from me.
So instead I gave him my soul,
which meant I was empty.
If only I could ask him if
my everything meant something.

I would have rowed a gondola

into the watery heart of Venice,
got down on one knee and confessed
an anthology of how my partner
makes me feel.

I'm relieved it was only an if.
It's a gift every morning I wake up.
I'm not going to be someone
that ends their life story with
plot holes.

Paradox

You have rolled smooth bed sheets
yet messy hair.
Shelves that home carefully placed DVD's
but pick'n'mix underwear.
The television screen is sparkling,
though there are empty
milk cartons everywhere.
Your love has been polished clean
So I don't mind kissing you anywhere.

Only you can love the mess
I leave behind.

One Day

To be honest I am scared of the world,
so I hide inside my poetry.
I wish my words could cuddle up
to the lonely and tell them I'm here.
If I was paid enough for my art I would
make hunger disappear and I'd
watch the starved laugh as they swallowed up
their fears.
My rhymes would make criminals think twice.
I would save them from being locked up
for the rest of their lives.

I dream one day my comma's
will provide the cure to cancer.
Put an end to illness full stop.
Every smoothly read stanza would
Bring water flowing into Africa.
My speech marks would mark
With permanent ink
my place in history.
Like Gandhi,
Martin Luther King.
Not for fame or recognition,
just to be remembered.
To show words are the
only thing
you need to change the game.

To change the world.

Lately the news has been miserable enough to

bring Mr Hyde from within me to write freely.
You're the big story everyone needs to be reading.
And they will,
but only when you need them to
as much as you need breathing.

Number 80

Everything will change number 80.
The sly movements of strange men
With camel humps full of stolen treasure,
do not tiptoe through your door anymore.
They tickle along the brass handle,
No longer feeling audacious
enough to enter.

Many pets will come to pass,
twice the amount of tears will be shed for them.
But don't lament something you have not yet loved.
Many more companions will come.

Your children have grown old enough now
to start searching for their own homes,
though their stories will be forever etched
into the bricks that make you.

The howls of dementia that soaked
Through the walls into your bedrooms
have silenced now.
Death was humane for this rare occasion
and put the werewolf out of his misery
with a silver bullet.

Bugs will no longer chose to have their
Funerals upon the glass of your windows.
Now sunlight can hijack the attic
and plant some bright ideas.

Queen Of The Deep

I've seen this girl with body language
That begs attention but a gaze that
Causes me to tense up.
She is only buying time so her
Loneliness doesn't leak through
Her clothes, but now she's spent up.
She hates gambling but she could
bet everything she owns that her
debt will still be standing
long after she is not.

She's a fish swimming in an
Ocean of wine and spirits even
though she's way under the age limit.
Her spirit is suffocated with every new
Breath, she's following the wrong school
Of fish that's heading for the
destination of an early death.
It's a shame the bags under her eyes
can't keep her above the raging waves.
I've offered her a life preserver but she
Didn't take it because she was too busy
Entertaining the sharks that circled her.

If she can find a way to the shore,
a desert island away from everything.
She may be able to find peace and serenity.
Hoping for popularity to ignite
a spark in her heart, she lit a flame.
Now she wonders why life is burning
through so quickly.
She only wanted to be the warmth
Everyone would cosy up to.
But now she feels like the London fire.

The Centre

Calling thousands of strangers
on a daily basis
is like throwing yourself into
shark infested waters
hoping to make friends.

Your electric words
escape down the line
as you pray when the charge
comes back
you don't burn inside.

The receivers shoot arrows
at the apple on your head,
sometimes they miss.
They puncture the wrong part
of you.
Anger bleeds from your

body until it falls into
an abyss of I don't cares.
Because smile as you dial
is what they tell you.

When your audience is faceless,
Your confidence must armour itself up
for battle without even a pen
to defend itself.

My own voice has taught me lessons.
How silence is an offering
for someone else to take control.
Open questions lead to open hearts.
And no matter how strong
Someone's defences are,
You can always identify the
crack in their walls
and break through.

Game Over

The tick of a clock or the click of a gun,
red eyed nights and stiff thumbs,
stinging corneas waiting for someone
to finally call it quits for the night.
Energy drinks clinking on the cabinet,
I'm thinking I should take it easy.
Tiredness is killing me,
Literally.
Ten times in a row.
My friends have become just voices

inside my headset.
Killing time is the only thing I feel
I'm any good at.

My screen is awake still but ignoring me,
I lay into a coffin and pull sheets onto a
fully clothed body.
The sunlight is bright slats now,
dawn cracks and hours pass.
How is it school time already?

The video game of my life is on a
difficulty level too high.
Forced to play the same mission
every single night.
There's probably some simple code
to unlock a way out of this endless cycle,
but I'm too bone idle to realise.
RESET:

The Price of Winter

If I could sell you winter,
would you buy it?
Able to erase the season as if it was a sketch
on a coffee stained piece of scrap paper.
Winter could be forgotten,
the whole idea of it melted away
from our memories.
Click the fingers and the
snowflakes could coat the pathways
with a fresh winter paste.

There would be no price.
There'd only be the cost of destroying
lives to make yours more desirable.
The wind may blow the condensation
of gratitude from few to warm your ears.
But the bitter cold would kill more people
than you would be doing a favour.

Imagine the world without any snow,
no such thing as a white Christmas.
You would never step into a
winter wonderland again.
Santa would catch the bus from
a bone dry north pole to deliver
the presents many years too late.

If winter rest in my hands,
I'd give it you.
My heart would eventually thaw,
But only when yours was frozen.

One Syllable Dinner

If me and you had a meal
I would gulp my words
If you failed to steal them in the first place.
You stole my heart, so it would make sense.
My grip would be tense on my fork.
You would not need to get me a drink,
I'd cry tears into the cup
And fill it to the brink.
All the dreams you owe me I have ground and

they take the place of the salt.
You have left me bone dry from all the nights
I spent hands tight as I prayed for you back in life.

No I won't do it.
Eat on your own.

The Proverb

There is a proverb.
From Hull, Hell or Halifax, good Lord deliver us.
God has probably plugged his ears.
These words were stammered a thousand
times into hands that act as a microphone
that only the Almighty hears.
Our laws have changed now.
We are born a different crowd.
Hell is a hard pill to swallow
filled with the bitter questions
like where, why, dare I ask how?
We have learnt to stamp our
sin into the ground only
to lay churches upon it.
These heavenly houses
are crowded by darkness.
Bibles are stuck preaching to the
brick walls they are stashed in.
From Hull, Hell or Halifax, good Lord deliver us.
I fear we no longer know where we are heading.

Humanity's Question

There's a force so strong it can break
grown men and make them cry as if
they're a dam and the brick work has
come loose.

When the ground catches me with
Its rock fingers,
The cuts from my hands bleed out
my weakness but I always find myself
back on my feet again.
Gravity gives in because against
this invisible power it will never win.

There's a question you'll ask at some point
In your life if you haven't already asked it.
But the truth is it's already been answered
for you even though it's still bound and
gagged inside your brain.
You've taken it hostage.

The answer to the question
is waiting in a baby's laughter
on a bus journey home when
you need cheering up.
It's in a song you know the
Lyrics to better than your
Own language, but one day
It will make you cry for no reason.
It's the thing you considered
a gift from a higher power
But then like waste you tossed

It into the closest bin because
It seemed to be rubbish
you'd made up.
Fabricated nonsense.

There is a stubborn parent waiting
Somewhere tapping a pen against
their chin wandering what should
come next in your life story.
This 'being' requires everything
You are before he unleashes
Anything you desire.
Because the entity desires you.

All the questions I've been
Begging for the answers to
have been sitting in my ears for years.
They've been knocking on the
Door to my brain but recently,
It must have lock-picked its
way in because it took
me completely by surprise.
I cried when I realised
It was actually him.

Spiders Of The Web

You're beautiful, did you know that?
Thanks, but stop lying to me. I'm fat!
Yeah but you got nice lips, why don't
you show me how well they can kiss.
See this is exactly why I don't trust boys,
you think girls are just sex toys.
Don't annoy me, go on 'cam and I'll
show you exactly how much of a man
I am.
I don't want to see whatever you want
to show me.
I'm blocking you immediately.
Have fun with other girls because I'm done.
You're hilarious,
precarious even.
But you don't have an option in this,
a few clicks and them pictures you thought
were a secret will be in a status.
Yeah you can delete it.
But gossip hungry people will see it,
download and screenshot.
I've got to admit,
you're a big girl but you're hot!
Or shall I just send the best ones straight
to your friends?
Okay I'll go on Skype in a minute.
I just need to wipe my tears
and go shut the door so none of
my family hears.
Awesome I like girls emotional,
I've got my pants off I'll
go and get some lotion.

You're sick and deserve to be arrested.
Shut up you're really testing my patience,
I'm fed up waiting now.
If your don't get your knickers down
I am going to go and bully that Emo kid
until he slits his arm or drowns himself.
That blood is on your hands,
are you starting to understand?
As much as I can.
But why destroy so many lives?
Never mind that,
stop the chit-chat.
Go on cam.

Cam turns on

Who are those men?
You were supposed to be alone
you whore!
Just wait a second there's
someone knocking on my door.

These men, are police men.
I asked them to come.
After you bullied my friend,
I was determined to see justice done.
I saw your online name,
the same one that popped up to my friend.
She ended her life because you pretended to
be in love with her,
then the pictures of her naked body
you took got retweeted and shared
around Twitter and Facebook.
Now the officers are there to arrest you.

They have all the evidence they need
so they won't bother with a confession.

chat ended

Those Who Stare

I see them everywhere,
those who stare.
They may be in my peripheral vision,
but they're there.

I wonder what they're thinking.
Are they amazed by my presence?
They look at me without even blinking.
My fingers are forced to iron the kink
out of my hair.
I swear that I care too much about
nonsense.
Problems that are all in my head.
Everything I want to think,
my brain autocorrects.
Like I got no intellect,
Practically every fact I know
I've stolen from the internet.
My face looks like I've been
shoved in a blender, I'm that ugly.
Weight watching is my new hobby,
because I'm starting to get a little chubby.

If I give people a beanstalk of
my pathetic fears to climb,

I find they have no
choice but to look down on me.

Some people believe the eyes are
a gateway to the soul.
I guess my soul must be made of gold.
The fountain of youth is inside me,
My goal is to never grow old.
The bones that form my body,
Will eventually tell the last chapter
of my story.
But what makes me who I am
Is injected with everlasting glory.

Those who stare are probably in a
strong current of a daydream.
But still my self-esteem is rising from me
like a steam train.
Vain is okay if you pinch it
like a grain of sand.
Hold a small dose in your hand.
Just enough for you to have the strength
to withstand any length of hurt
that today has planned.

So before I let my confidence crack,
Maybe they're staring because
I'm staring back.

Imposter

Ghosts haunt the ghostly gaunt figures.
I've figured, because the residents of our town
did not host fulfilling enough lives.
The dust from their bodies have scattered wide.
Are you just a stranger living inside
a reoccurring dream?
Do you feel like you never have
anything real to hold onto?
Now your mistakes have hold on you.

You've thrown out the blueprints
to your own existence,
You've no idea of where to start building.
Laying bricks not to reinforce your goals,
but to stop any unrealistic ideas
escaping the hole in your logic
just to be shot down by the world.

You are strong and desire to exist.
If you fell off a cliff you'd hang on.
But you remain someone, the world
Will forget to miss when you're gone.
You possess so much talent
That people are jealous enough
to strangle your future.

Don't be a ghost,
You're just an imposter
in a white sheet.

Twisted Heart

My emotions are scrabbled.
When love ends hate begins.

L

O

V

HATE

I guess all the H's never stapled
to our agreement.
Happiness
Honesty
Heaven.
But you never planned to
stick around.
Did you?
I wish you were written on paper
so I could erase your mistakes and
Draw you back into my life.
But you're just a love poem
drowning in my irises.
You tossed your promises into
troubled water.
But you didn't stick around
for its rippled effect.

Slave To Poetry

When you're a metaphor magician words start
to cocoon themselves and transform into pictures.
But I tried magic on and it didn't fit me.
Self-esteem came to sit with me,
bashed sense into my head and said
my forte is poetry.

- Just hold on a second, Joel -

It wasn't Mr Esteem that came to your rescue,
You just allowed me the chance to breathe
now I take over everything.
It's all me,
I'm the demon inside your poetry.
The one giving you hints,
whispering you similes.
I could literally take death out
of your breath.
But I don't want to.

You try to ram memories
down readers throats.
Plus you actually want
them to give a damn, now that's a joke.

Nobody wants to know that
you never understood the world.
How you see the 2D version of life,
Or that *Christ* has made you convert.
They don't give a damn that you were hit by
A cricket bat when you were younger.

Or that you hunger for a poem
to hit home for somebody.
Your parents got divorced and
you were forced to live
with your father.
It must suck somebody stole your car,
drove it far and then blew it up.
Your life was stuck in a rut.
You struggled to find friends.
It was hard to close your eyes
And defend yourself from nightmares.

But guess what?
Nobody cares.

Here's the deal.
I'll let you steal you back your
writing freedom.
You can go back conjuring up the black
and white images you used to bore
your readers with.
But only if you burn every poem
before anyone gets the chance to see them.
Don't try and defy your own demons,
we're all you've got nowadays.

Voices

Now his voice sounds like an
abandoned time machine,
it used to keep me on edge
every time I listened in.
But now it's rusting and
can't reach 88mph so it
Fails to do anything
spectacular.

Every time I spoke to him
my breath would harden
and fall to the ground as
if it was unworthy to be
heard by anyone,
let alone him.

But now I realise I
was just charging his
pride off my own
batteries.
I see him and everything
Is somehow different.
An icicle hangs above
Us both with the potential
to do so much damage
but he can always manage
to melt it before everything
comes crashing down.

Time Warp

When I was younger I used to hunger for
my Dad and Mum to get back together.
I couldn't understand that their happily
ever after marriage was never going
to last forever.
I dreamed that I could go back.
Time travel.
Watch the years unravel the tight knots
in my throat so I could tell them both
how I really felt.
Was I too young to even know myself?
Maybe I would have slipped a note on
my bedroom shelf saying all the positive
things that would happen in future.
My Mum would browse through it
when she was lonely and had nothing else
to do but to get drunk and wander into every room,
hoping for the darkness to cuddle her.
Depression loves company.

I can't say that nothing good has come
out of this disaster,
I just wish it had come faster.
I've mastered my past and transformed
it into my strength.
But the lengths my mum went through
to overcome what needed to was intense.
I'm not blaming my Dad for anything he's done,
Even though it was wrong it has made me stronger
than I ever would have become.

So I guess time is my friend.
But even still I won't pretend these events never happened.
All the happiness I know now would escape out of the
window.
What I would have become if I could change the past
 I will never know.
Though I am able to alter the future
even if it is a bumpy and unpredictable road.

Jump

You jump into my arms like a leap of faith.
It makes me jump out of my skin,
Suddenly I feel naked to the bone so
I jump back in.
When I see you my eyes jump from my face,
keep them in your purse
so they can see you through the day
and warn you when you're not
spending your life living it to the fullest.
I want you to jump into my dreams
So even when the sun hides
behind the hills,
I don't have to bribe the night
To jump back into day.
I've never felt love this quickly,
It jumped out like a jack in the box
And hit me.
My heart engine has shut down.
Would you mind jump starting it back to
life before I fill it with your
Love poison?

Coming Home

My bedroom door was my kingdom's gate
except no riches waited for me on the other side.
An attic ladder led me to my heaven.
Once I was there no problems could reach me,
Like God cast them away before they
had change to breach the peace.
But before I'd get there I would have to
pass the elephant in the living room that
used to suck up the atmosphere and
attention when I scraped the guilt off
my shoes and stamped it into the carpet.
Now it's clear enough to dance on,
I'll have to let my memories sing
A song I once knew.

People used to say that nothing
would faze me.
They couldn't place me into any
Social category because I was a weird
kind of crazy.
I'd do the same things over and over
and get different results.

Hiking thoughts that walked all over blank pages
are the only things that left home with me.
I used to go on quests when I was desperate to find jobs
but the dragons behind their desks would spit fire in my
face before I had even stepped into their territories.
I'd crawl up the piano key steps playing the blues because
I would always lose the piano sheets in dark times.

But now when I face my bedroom door it still
feels like a kingdom's gate.
If you sit on my throne and wait for me,
I'll have all the riches I need.

Best Seller

You've ripped up all the photos
that we ever had of you and me.
You used to drink every night,
it made you forget the reality
of what had eventually come
when your belief was mentally done.
and you think you lost the war.
How can you not see you've actually won?

You were worse than Kryptonite,
because I died
every time I tried
to not think about you.
Because all I wanted to do
was hold you tight.
The rope that tied my heart
to yours had been sliced.
My body grew weaker
every single night,
you were my emotional exercise.

I was like a pied piper,
all the snakes were
hissing in my ear.
Filling plot holes.

When your body occupies
a lost soul,
fear grabs the wheel
because you don't know
where to steer.

The worst mistakes
make the best stories.
I guess you're going to
be a best seller.

Monument

A forgotten monument has fallen out with time.
Once it would have been beautiful but now the
Name and description has been erased
from the face of it.
Mould forms like green grapes.
Its only friend is a maze.
Tall enough to lose a small child.
As the days flick away my age
locks me in a cage. I can never have as much
fun as I used to. Now after dark is the only time
I can discover my inner child. The stars look bright
tonight and I'm feeling in the right mood to recite
some poetry to the guardians that watch over me.
Wildlife jumps out of the non-fiction books, animals
wander the nature trails in the comfort of corrupt
shadows that shield their wild ways. In the earlier
days of the park, the masterpiece would've been
happy to call the land around it home. But now it's
just a monument consigned to oblivion, standing alone.

Libraryology

Look that word up in the dictionary,
I dare you.
You know it will be playing hide and seek
amid the paper pages of the present.
Words are viruses infecting us.
We catch them by listening to others
speaking the words they have heard from
somebody else.
We pull language from our knowledge backpacks
when it suits a purpose.
Libraryology is just a baby I gave birth to
so it suited mine...

Snap my word in two,
I dare you.
Library-ology,
The definition of library is a room containing
Cupid's family that shoot arrows at your heart
every time you pick up a book.
Library - that place you enter someone else's
imagination.
Library - a building that shelves dead people's
lives which you can revive just by
reading the first page.
Ology - a subject of study,
a branch of knowledge in your forest of interests.

Define Libraryology,
I dare you.
The study of writers becoming immortal.
The study of the fight between books and technology.

The study of why you can never get library books back on time.

Words come and go.
But they make us who we are today.
Libraryology – the study of how people die
but their words live on.

Rising

I
wish we
could unite in
our old school,
but that's impossible
because everything's new.
I planted my childhood memories
in a time capsule that I hoped one day
we'd dig up. We'd be baffled by the way we
calmed the volcano erupting inside us when exam
time came.
I can picture
telling those
who made my
life hell just
how cold the
flames are now.
I'm stuck in the
clouds, only
Looking down
to see how far
I've come.

Raining Thank Yous

If I said thanks to all the people who truly deserve it,
my throat would run dry like sandpaper and scratch
all the meaning from my words until only the
shavings are left to be spat out at you.
Individually you mean that much to me I could
polish you down and put you on my shelf
because you're the reason for
my biggest achievements.

There are some of you that have written to me
and acted as if my poetry was a present.
Almost as if I'd stuffed my stanzas into a box
and given them to you personally for your birthday.

Thank you.

I hope the people who have shone a spotlight on me
will identify their names in between
the lines of this stanza,
the ones that opened their ears to devour any poem
I have shoved in their faces as if time and space
would implode if I didn't get to show it right that second.

Thank you.

Some of you have even sliced time
from your own schedules for me.
Precious moments you could have spent
chasing your own dreams but instead
you offered it to me so I could succeed.
Now like a jigsaw every piece has come
together and I see the whole picture.

Thank you.

There are four people that deserve
a lot more thanks than I can give.
My Dad has been a line connecting all the
dots for me even though the possibility
of me achieving was next to zero.
I spoke about you harshly Dad but
deep down you'll always be my hero.

The editor of *The Courier* has gathered all
The doubts about my ability and pressed delete.
He's shown me that it doesn't matter how
young you are, you are always worth a read.

Without my publisher these words could
have never landed in your hands.
What I owe this man I don't think
he will ever understand.

One day I received a random email
and I still have no idea
how it even got to me.
It invited me to a place where
a talented woman would inject
me with poetry.
Then as they say –
the rest is history.

Thank you.